Patterns Around the World

Emily Ballinger

People weave rugs that have patterns.

What patterns do you see in this rug?

People make beadwork that has patterns.

What patterns do you see in this beadwork?

People sew quilts that have patterns.

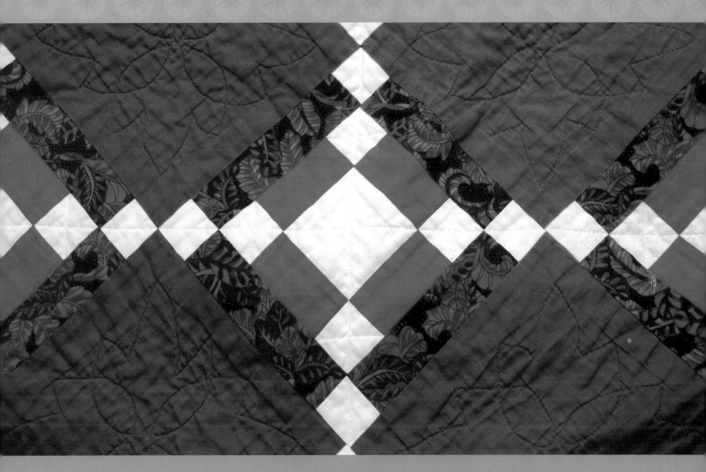

What patterns do you see in this quilt?

People make baskets that have patterns.

What patterns do you see in this basket?

People make pictures that have patterns.

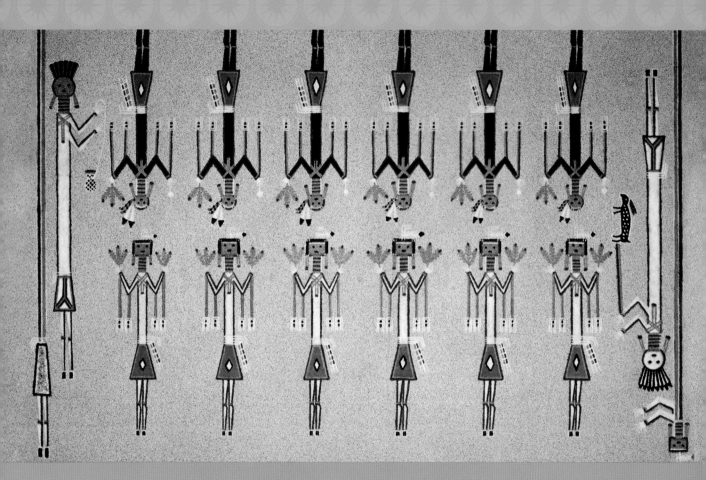

What patterns do you see in this picture?

11

Patterns make our world more interesting!